PASSING POINT

1868 Steamboat Collision on the Ohio River

On the cover: B&W engraving by E. P. Frazer from Harper's Weekly, December 26, 1868, of the collision of the *United States* and the *America.*

By Don Morrison

© 2017

This trade paperback original is published by:
Donmo Publications
2102 Sylvan Circle
Maryville, TN 37803

True story of the collision of the steamers *United States* and *America* on the Ohio River on December 4, 1868, one of the worst river disasters in U. S. history.

Manufactured in the United States of America

Printed by CreateSpace

First Edition: August 2017

ISBN 978-0-9855925-2-3

Library of Congress Cataloging-In-Publication Data

Morrison, Don 1938 –

Passing Point: 1868 Steamboat Collision on the Ohio River, by Don Morrison © 2017, First Ed.

1. Steamboat Collisions, 1868   2. Steamers *United States* and *America*   3. Ohio River Steamboat Accidents
Title: Passing Point

Cover and text formatting: Linda Weaver

Author photo on back cover: Wynn Goodchild

Contents

Illustrations:

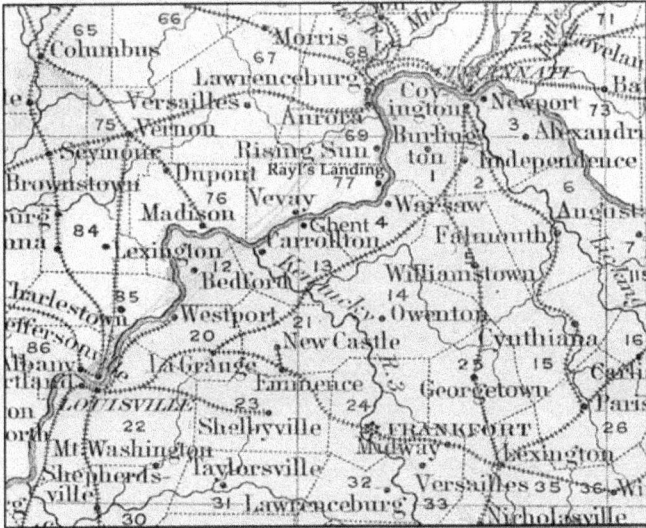

**Author's 1871 Map of the Ohio River
from Louisville up to Cincinnati
where the steamers *United States* and *America*
operated in 1868.**

The steamboat *United States*, circa 1868, from the
article "Glimpses into the Past on the Ohio River,"
by Dr. Carl Bogardus, 1977. From the top: 1. Pilot house; 2.
Texas, where officers and crew had their sleeping quarters;
3. Small skylights above the large cabin where the dance
took place; 4. Stateroom doors and windows, with removable
shutters, surrounding the cabin; and 5. Freight deck.

*This book is dedicated to the memory
of the many victims of this
tragic accident.*

Prelude

On the afternoon of December 4th, 1868, Marcus Toney bought a ticket from Cincinnati down to Louisville on the steamer *United States*. The *United States*, like her sister boat, the *America*, was a state-of-the-art steamboat in the evening trade between Cincinnati and Louisville on the Ohio River. Both of these wooden-hulled boats were built and owned by the U. S. Mail Line Company, based in Cincinnati. One of the sisters embarked from Cincinnati every evening and the other left Louisville, so that they passed during the night, usually near Rayl's Landing on the Indiana side not far from the village of Florence, Indiana, and across from the larger town of Warsaw, Kentucky. These large steamers made no landings on the way except at Lawrenceburg and Madison, both on the Indiana side. Together these boats were the most formidable rivals of the railroads at that time. As boats became larger and steamboat trade on the Ohio became more competitive after the war, and as more of the obstacles in the river were removed, the larger boats no longer tied up at the shore at night, but continued on their way throughout the hours of darkness. At five-thirty in the evening, the *United States*, which had been in service for two-and-a-half years, was scheduled to cast off her lines from the wharfboat at the foot of Vine Street in Cincinnati.

Wharfboat at Cincinnati by Jacob Gervis, as it appeared in *Harper's Weekly*, June 12, 1869

Wharfboats were used as staging platforms for loading and unloading steamboats. A boat was needed for the purpose, rather than a fixed wharf, because it could rise and fall with the river stage, just as the boats did. Large ports like Cincinnati and Louisville built huge wharfboats that equaled the size of large steamboats. Smaller river towns built more modest structures for freight handling, and some of the lesser steamboat stops were likely to use wharfboats repurposed from steamboats that had gone out of service. The worn or damaged bows and sterns were cut off and bulkheaded up. Weak places were patched and the interiors stripped to become cavernous bays for the staging of freight to be onloaded to, and offloaded from, packet boats, which were steamers that carried freight, mail, and passengers. Each small port of call up and down the river had its own version of a wharfboat. A pilot who could land a big wind-catching steamboat alongside one of these structures in bad weather without sinking his steamer, the wharfboat, or both, won the admiration of the kids and old men who hung about the wharf at river towns along the way.

At the Cincinnati Mail Line wharfboat, deckhands, usually Irishmen or Negroes, carried the freight from an arriving boat onto the wharfboat and stacked it in piles, or tiers, so that it could be loaded onto drays and hauled away. When the incoming freight had been unloaded, the rousters would start reloading the boat.

In preparation for the reloading, a procession of big four-wheel drays from warehouses of the shipping companies came down the bank and onto the wharfboat. These drays had low, heavy wooden wheels with iron tires and were drawn by teams of draft horses. The noise from many of these drays rolling over the rough cobblestone levy could drown out other wharfside sounds. They rumbled up across the wooden landing stage and into the wharfboat, the horses' hooves thumping on the uneven oak planks. The deckhands, if they were Negroes, would often break into a coonjine, or rhythmic song, that gave their work a cadence and provided a diversion for boarding passengers.

While the loading was in progress, the passengers began to arrive, Marcus Toney among them. He stood at the rail a few minutes, back to the wind, collar of his heavy coat turned up, black bowler hat clamped on his head and gloves protecting his hands from the freezing metal railing. He looked down on the bustling beehive below as the drays came down making their deafening way across the rough levy, and roustabouts transferred their heavy loads from the wharfboat onto the steamer. The young man drew a deep breath and tried to parse the myriad odors that wafted over the waterfront in the swirling wind. The redolence of hot grease from supper cooking in the wharfside eateries and the smell of coal smoke from the banked fireboxes of the *United States* were easy to identify. All of it was overlaid with the stench of waste from the slaughterhouses that was routinely dumped into the river. Even these foul smells brought a smile to Mr. Toney's face. It was good to be traveling, seeing new things, noticing sights and sounds he hadn't really considered in years, and without thoughts of the recent war and prison on his mind. He relished the idea that at the end of his journey he would be home in Nashville visiting his parents and siblings. For him life was becoming normal again. He had a good job, and he was looking forward to a few days off.

Soon tiring of the blustery wind and rain, Marcus went down the stairs to watch freight being loaded onto the lower deck by the rousters and deckhands. The inside of the wharfboat was especially gloomy on this December evening. Twilight had come early and the interior of the place was lighted only by coal oil lanterns swinging from above. Outside on the river the cold wind whipped up angry whitecaps, and gusts swept in the open doors of the wharfboat. The freight clerk hustled about his duties in a long, heavy overcoat and a hat that came down over his ears. He warmed his fingers with his breath.

Oliver Noble, the mate, could be heard above the din and clatter roaring his orders to the rousters and deckhands. People unversed in the ways of steamboat men thought he was overbearing, but he was expert in the use of mate's English and the laborers thought him eloquent.

Inside the lower deck of the *United States,* deck hands took the freight from the rousters who carried, dragged, or rolled it on board. Among the cargo being loaded were twenty-five or thirty wooden barrels, painted blue and marked "coal oil." The barrels were rolled over the steel plate at the lower end of the wooden stage and up into the boat. This type of freight had to be carried in a place with good air circulation, so the barrels were headed up, and some of them stowed in single tiers outside the baggage room of the boat. Others were stowed in a single tier on the forecastle, some eight feet forward of the front steps to the upper deck, and near the capstan.

Mr. Toney noticed other passengers arriving. Out-of-town travelers came down in horse-drawn hacks from the Spencer House, the Burnet House, and smaller hotels. Wealthy Cincinnatians came in their own carriages drawn by beautiful horses made more spirited by the chilly weather. Homeward bound shoppers from smaller downriver towns trudged down over the levy on foot. There were no crowds coming down to wish their kinfolk and associates goodbye and to linger until the boat departed. On this winter evening only the passengers' closest friends and family braved the miserable weather.

Up in the boat's office, Purser Robert Riley was on hand to greet the passengers and to assign them their staterooms. Riley was quite popular, personally acquainted with many of the businessmen passengers from Cincinnati, Louisville, and Madison. He looked up to see his friends, Captain John Scott and his wife, both well known around Cincinnati.

The Scotts had brought a couple of ladies down to embark on the *United States*, Mrs. Nellie Jones, a youthful-appearing lady and a cousin of the Scotts, along with her daughter, Eva, about twenty and also good-looking. Mother and daughter were from Pensacola, Florida. The Scotts put the two ladies under the care of another cousin, Captain Joe McCammant, for the trip down to Louisville.

Shortly after the Scotts bade the Jones ladies goodbye, fifty-two-year-old Captain Richard Wade tapped the big bell on the roof, and the Negro deckhands, called "darkies" by the boat's officers, dragged the lines back on board. Jacob Remlein was on watch in the pilot house. He signaled the engine room from the bellstand and maneuvered the *United States* slowly away from the wharfboat. He stepped on the whistle treadle, sending echoes of the departure signal rolling out over the dark lowlands. He rounded the vessel to and proceeded downriver under full steam. The boat clerk's list showed 168 passengers and crew on board, but due to the foul weather, not all who had bought tickets actually boarded for Louisville.

To the few hardy souls who stayed on the waterfront to see the departure of the *United States*, she was soon lost in darkness. Likewise, to Marcus Toney and the others on the boat the shore line made a pale presentation with only the oil-fueled street lights and lamps glowing dimly from windows to be seen through the murky rain and darkness.

Dropping down the river, battling the headwind at a speed of twelve to fifteen miles per hour, the *United States* passed Sedamsville, edged by the dark shadows of the hills behind Modoc Bar, and on past the mouth of the Big Miami River.

At Lawrenceburg, she put in and picked up a shipment of whiskey in wooden barrels. They were rolled up the stage and set head-up on the forecastle next to the coal oil barrels. The rain was now freezing on the decks. The deckhands howled as the wind drove the stinging drops against their faces. Oliver Noble's harsh voice urged the men to speed up their work. There was no coonjine during this loading.

After leaving a landing, Noble would often go up to visit with the pilot, but he had his little boy, Lon, making the trip with him. He was up in the Texas, asleep in his father's room. The Texas was the top deck just below the pilot house where some of the officers and crew had their sleeping quarters. These top decks began to appear on new steamboats around 1845, the year Texas was admitted to the Union, whence the name. Oliver went up to the Texas, joined his son, and turned in for the night. Down in the baggage room Elijah Forte, a Negro porter, snoozed in a large chair. He'd experienced a boiler explosion on the *General Lytle* two years ago. After that experience he took out a $6,000 life insurance policy and kept it paid up.

One observer noted that this night was "dark as a dungeon" and "the wind had fangs." Pilot Jake Remlein drove the prow of the United States into the heavy swells rolling up the reach, or channel, below Aurora. She shuddered as her lead plowed into the waves. River captains and pilots say December nights are the blackest and longest of the year. And no nights are darker or lonelier, they say, than nights up in that glass cage with the wind driving rain against the window panes, high up above the unseen muddy waters of the river, no path visible ahead, no shoreline in sight, just the inky shadows of the hills. A steamboat pilot needed to know the river, her moods, her depths, her winding course, like a horse knows his way home at night.

The captain knew that on the deck below the Texas, in the staterooms, most of the passengers were sleeping, trusting his skill and steady hand. In the high-ceilinged cabin on the same deck a dance was in progress. Two bridal couples had been discovered on board and a celebration was arranged in their honor. One couple was elderly, the other young.

Four thrones were set up at the back of the ladies' cabin for the newlyweds using an arrangement of chairs covered with tapestry provided by the cabin crew. A magician gave an impromptu exhibition of his skill, and an Italian orchestra, employed by the Mail Line, played favorite songs of the day and waltzes that brought dancers to the floor. Melodies wafted through the long cabin, and the crystal chandeliers with crimson shades provided a soft glow from frescoed beams overhead. The dancers bowed as they passed the two honored couples.

Marcus Toney noticed that all eyes of the passengers were on two beautiful girls in the ballroom that night. They nearly stole the limelight from the brides, and the young men lined up to dance with them. One of the ladies was a Madison girl, Mary Johnson, the beloved daughter of Colonel A.Y. Johnson. Col. Johnson had sent Mary's cousin, Lewis Johnson, to Cincinnati to accompany his long-absent daughter on the last leg of her journey home. Mary had been introduced to Eva Jones during the wedding celebration. They quickly became friends and were the belles of the evening. Eva's mother, Nellie, sat on the sidelines with Joe McCammant.

Captain Wade came down from the pilothouse to preside over the festivities, leaving pilot Jake Remlein at the wheel. Along the side, businessmen were seated in little groups discussing the topics of the day, and a small group of men from Madison stood in the gangway near the barber shop watching the gay proceedings and talking casually to each other. Marcus Toney joined this group.

Mr. Toney listened to the conversation and watched the other young people whirling and stepping spritely on the ballroom floor. He saw Mary Johnson and Eva Jones coming toward him, chatting happily as they returned from the powder room. One of the Madison men mentioned Mary's name to the others when they saw the girls approaching. Marcus smiled and bowed slightly as the girls passed. His eyes followed them as they made their way onto the dance floor and were immediately engaged in bright conversation by two young gents.

Captain Wade looked toward the windows of the salon and out into the darkness. A barely discernable look of apprehension crept into his eyes just before he turned and graciously took leave of the three ladies who had been speaking with him. He then stepped outside and went up on the roof to look things over. What he saw did not encourage him. The black clouds overhead had turned gray, indicating the moon had risen, but visibility had not improved.

The captain had consulted his almanac and knew tonight's moon had risen at 8:22 PM, would set at 11:40 AM the next day, and that it was a three-quarter moon, in the waning gibbous stage and three days past full. Were it not for the heavy cloud cover, the visibility would have been quite good, but the mist and rain and gray conditions made it difficult for the pilot and captain to judge distances accurately. In spite of the weather, pilot Remlein and the pilot in training, Bill Turpin, seemed to have things under control, so the captain returned to the festivities below. The other pilot, John Hamilton, was resting in his room in the

Texas. He was due to go on duty in the pilot house in a little less than an hour, at eleven o'clock.

Below in the engine room, Charles Marshall was in charge of the watch. He had his engines working smoothly, rolling the big wheels over with that uneven rhythm peculiar to sidewheelers. The boat pushed into the wind and down past Patriot, a village on the Indiana side. Charles's brother, Chief Engineer Arrin Marshall, was asleep in the Texas, also due to come on duty at eleven.

Some railroad men among the passengers complained to Captain Wade that the noise of the party outside their doors so late at night was keeping them awake. The hands of the big clock in the cabin pointed to half past ten. Captain Wade then stopped the entertainment, and most of the revelers retired to their rooms.

෨

The other boat, *America*, was upbound from Louisville that night. The clerk's list showed 192 passengers and crew, but as with her sister boat at

Cincinnati, not all ticketholders came aboard because of the bad weather. Built at Cincinnati in 1867, she was even newer, larger, and finer than the *United States*. Together the magnificent sister boats had cost a half-million dollars, and were insured for half their construction costs. From the 1820s to 1868, the Mail Line Company had prospered without the loss of a single boat, a marvelous record.

In the early days of steamboat navigation, beginning in the teens and early twenties of the 19th Century, individuals and small companies built and ran steamboats. Some of these were poorly constructed, and they operated with unskilled crews. Owners' greed for quick profits and the reckless nature of the captains accounted for many steamboat accidents. In those early days, the western rivers were full of snags and other uncharted obstacles, which were deadly hazards for boats. Also, fires, boiler explosions, and collisions resulted in gruesome accidents. There were few navigation regulations until years later. In view of these facts, it was remarkable that the U. S. Mail Line, which began packet boat operation in 1820, was able to compile such an exemplary safety record.

During the Civil War, packet boat service was interrupted. The Union Army pressed many steamboats into war service. They were part of General-in-Chief Winfield Scott's "Anaconda Plan," on rivers and coastlines ringing the Confederacy, whereby the Southern forces were blockaded against naval imports by the Union's stronger navy. Some of the commandeered steamers were used to transport supplies and ammunition, and others were outfitted as rams and gunboats. When the war ended, the U. S. Mail Line saw the need for even larger and faster boats for the civilian trade, so they built the *United States* and the *America*.

Among the notable passengers on the *America* that evening, as she prepared to cast off from Louisville, was the celebrated Norwegian violinist Ole Bull and his troupe of musicians. They were scheduled to give a concert at Cincinnati the next evening at Pike's Music Hall. Mr. Christopher G. Pearce, president of the Mail Line Company, was also on board. He had been captain and pilot on riverboats for thirty years. Another steamboat man, Captain Charles Nichols, of Covington, Kentucky, was a passenger on the America headed for Cincinnati that evening.

The *America* had a very sharp prow with an iron covering tightly attached over her bow and on down to her bottom where it extended toward her stern as far back as her sidewheels. Captain David Whitten was her master. He had been on the river over forty years, for part of that time commanding gunboats on the Mississippi during the war.

The two regular pilots on the *America* were Charles Ditman of Jeffersonville, Indiana, and Charles Dufour of Ghent, Kentucky. A few days previous to this, Dufour had gone home for a few days on a short leave, and Napoleon Jenkins came on board to relieve him for three round trips. Jenkins would stand watch in the pilot house until eleven PM, when Ditman would take over.

Jenkins, though an experienced pilot, was an elderly man and a substitute pilot for occasions such as this. He had been in trouble three years earlier, when the *Major Anderson*, which Jenkins was piloting, collided with the *St. Charles* at Cooper's Bar below Hanover, Indiana. As a result of that accident, his license and that of John Hamilton of Vevay, who was on watch with him at the time, were suspended for thirty days. Napoleon Jenkins was also illiterate, which may not have enhanced his credentials as a pilot.

At the appointed hour that evening, Captain Whitten tapped the bell and the lines were thrown off. With much "scaping" of spent steam, Jenkins eased the *America* away from the Louisville wharfboat and she was soon on her way up the river. With the west wind pushing her broad stern and her smoke blowing straight out in front of her she might have been making ten miles per hour against the current, or a little more when running directly before the wind. When she reached Grassy Flats, seventeen miles above Louisville, the wind became stronger, and on past Eighteen Mile Island, Westport, and Bethlehem it continued unabated. From there on up to Madison the country was very dark on that cloudy winter night. The hillsides, which in some places come right down to the water's edge, were heavily wooded and farmhouses were few. In 1868 there were no headlights on the boats and no autos with lights on riverside roads.

The *America's* superstructure stood high above the water like a sail, which caused the boat to slide away from the channel when the wind hit her broadside in the bends. Up in the creaking glass pilot house it took all of Jenkins's skill to keep her in the channel. Boats like the sisters *America* and *United States* were shallow-drafted and flat-bottomed, having no keels to steady them against the wind.

Down in the engine room, Engineer James Holmes watched his gauges. The cook house was closed after dinner was served, but there was food on the galley table for night lunches for the crew. In the office the freight clerk was balancing his books under the amber glow of a shaded coal oil lamp. Groups of men sat around in the passenger cabin and swapped yarns. Mr. Pearce, president of the Mail Line, had retired to his room, no doubt secure in his knowledge that his company had the best boats, officers, and crews on the river.

Ole Bull, a gregarious man, chatted with his new friends at the bar, having introduced himself by properly pronouncing his name as "Ol-uh Bool," not "Old Bull," as some Americans called him. They told him tales of the river and legends of the many boats that had burned or were sunk by snags or storms. They spoke of others destroyed by boiler explosions, such as the *Moselle* at Cincinnati in April, 1838 and the *Lucy Walker* below New Albany in October, 1844. In this disaster, large pieces of iron were hurled out over bordering cornfields and human bodies were torn asunder.

The Norwegian violinist said he did not fear storms or accidents, but that tonight he would follow his usual custom. When traveling on boats or the cars, he said, he always slept in his clothes in order to be prepared for a hasty exit if the need arose.

Madison came into view, not the modern town with its electric lights, but the ancient Madison, shrouded by dark hills, and with its dim candles and coal oil lamps. After the routine stop at Madison, Jenkins's sidewheeler continued upriver, powering past Brooksburg, Carrollton, and Vevay. Along this stretch of the river there were broader and more frequent bottomlands between the river and bordering hills. These places were not regular landing points for the grand sister steamers. Cincinnati, Madison, and Louisville packets, smaller boats, made these villages.

With Neb Jenkins still at the wheel, the America moved on up past Warsaw. One writer characterized this section of the river with the understatement, "The channel was somewhat devious at this point." (See the map of this area, page 62.)

The pilot pulled the head of the *America* out as she approached the wreck of the sternwheeler *Tom Scott*, sunk in 1863. Large boils in the water marked the wreck site, near the lower end of the place where the channel crossed over to the Indiana side toward Rayl's Landing.

It was in this same double bend of the river that the *Telegraph* collided with the brand new *Kentucky Home* in 1855, and sank her. Also, the *Lady Walton* and the *Norman* collided and sank here. If those weren't sufficient hazards for pilots, add to these obstacles a sunken barge and a large bar with exposed rocks at the mouth of Bryant's Creek on the Indiana side.

Ahead, Jenkins saw dim lights of a steamboat coming down as he made the crossing. He later stated that he did not see the signal lights of the *United States*, only the lights from her cabin and furnace doors. He judged the lights to be about two miles distant, and he soon made out the ghostly form of the *United States* approaching. He judged she was making about twelve miles an hour. The stage of the river at this point was about seventeen feet in the channel.

Captain David Whitten was in the pilot house with Jenkins. When the pilot recognized the approaching lights he remarked to the captain, "Yonder comes Uncle Dick now," meaning Captain Richard Wade of the *United States*.

Pilot Remlein on the *United States* said he saw the signal lights and the lights from the cabin and fire doors of the *America* at about the same time. He steered down the channel, which here favored the Indiana side and was straight and about 400 yards wide on down to Rayl's Landing. From there the channel crossed to the Kentucky side where the *America* was then crossing, coming up.

The *America* completed the crossing, and Jenkins had her straightened up with the Indiana shore, about a hundred yards out. He said he believed the *United States* to be a little farther out from the Indiana shore, and coming straight down. He judged the boats were about a mile apart when he blew two long and distinct whistles about three seconds apart, and at the same time gave the *America* the wheel toward the left, or Indiana shore.

By Rule One of the steamboat navigation manual, when two boats prepare to pass, the upbound boat must signal first as to which side she wishes to pass on, one whistle if she intends to pass to her right, two if to the left. Having sounded two whistles, Jenkins announced his intention to pass the *United States* between her and the Indiana shore.

But the regular-duty pilots of the two steamers had a long-standing, unfailing routine for passing each other when they met near Rayl's Landing. Always the upbound boat kept to the Kentucky side of the channel, and the downbound steamer hugged the Indiana shore. What Jake Remlein, pilot of the *United States*, did not know was that the *America's* regular pilot was not on duty this night. Neb Jenkins decided to pass the downbound boat in his own way, which was actually his prerogative, according to Rule One.

Pilot Remlein had expected the ascending boat to signal for sides by blowing her whistle, but he grew impatient when the signal from the *America* did not come as early as he thought necessary. This observation was possibly due to the poor visibility on this "gray night." Consequently, Remlein signaled first, giving his customary one sound of his whistle, indicating he would take the Indiana side.

Unfortunately, at the instant Remlein sounded his one whistle, it evidently coincided perfectly with the first of two whistles from the *America*. Thus, hearing only the second sound blown by the *America*, and supposing he had received one whistle in answer, he came ahead. But when he saw the *America* steer toward the Indiana side, he immediately rang his engineer to stop and back his engines. By the time the wheels of the *United States* had made only three or four revolutions in backing, Remlein saw it was too late.

Jenkins said later that he had the *America* going up the channel about where he wanted her to be, and the *United States* was coming down in the position he expected. Then he said, "The signal I heard from the *United States* was one whistle, which meant she wanted to take the same side I was taking. But the *United States* was to the right of me and less than a mile up the river." Jenkins blew two whistles again, and rang the bells to stop the engines and back them strong. By then the boats were too close together, and the consequences were unavoidable.

Captain Whitten went to the front of the *America's* pilot house, opened the window, and shouted at the *United States*, though he could not be heard at that distance, "Where are you going! Stop that boat!" No reply was heard from the *United States*. Less than two minutes later the boats collided.

Collision

Captain Whitten hurried down on the roof from the pilothouse of the *America* just before the two boats crashed. When they collided, the only damage done to the *America* was that her jackstaff was knocked down. Captain Whitten ran behind one of the chimneys to avoid being hit as it fell. He came out from behind the chimney and directed Jenkins to run the *America* in to the Indiana shore, which he did. When the *America* struck the front of the *United States* she climbed up three or four feet on her forecastle. The razor-sharp ironclad prow of the *America* had struck the *United States* on her port side a few feet from her bow and cut into her wooden forecastle deck and the cross timbers that supported it. The *United States* was nearly cut in two on a diagonal of some thirty-six feet, forcing some of the planking off her starboard side. The *America's* prow crashed through the baggage room, which on steamboats was always under the main stairway near the bow, and finally came to rest there. Elijah Forte was killed instantly as he slept in his chair. The America then backed out and settled back in the water at her sister's bow. She vibrated from stem to stern, then continued backing toward the Indiana shore.

With her engines in reverse and backing strong, the *America* left a ragged triangular opening from the forecastle deck down to the bottom of the *United States*. The two tiers of wooden barrels of coal oil and whiskey in the path of the *America's* prow burst and splintered, their contents pouring down over the deck and under the bulkhead and coal box toward the fireboxes.

The sweating firemen had been feeding the fireboxes. Parts of the furnaces glowed cherry red, as if they had just come out of a forge. The bulkhead behind the men hid the approaching *America* from their view, and when the collision came, they staggered and fell. They had no time to save themselves before the oil and whiskey reached the furnace and engulfed them in flames.

The fumes from the hot volatile liquids rushed ahead, and a raging fire rose up on the forward deck.

The cargo of both steamers included other flammable materials such as cotton, hay, brooms, and bacon. In seconds the entire forward cabin of the *United States* was an inferno, the flames leaping as high as the tops of her chimneys. An excited person opened the front door of the cabin. The flames rushed in with a roar and went hissing on down through the cabin. Some passengers were trampled and cremated on the spot, while others were fortunate enough to get outside on the guards and gain a little time.

Guards on a steamboat were extensions of the main deck out from the hull. They were originally adopted for sidewheel steamers to protect the paddle wheels and to provide a mounting point for the outer ends of the paddle wheel axles. The main deck planking extended out over the guards, and when a steamboat was fully loaded, riding deep in the water, it often appeared that the edges of the guards marked the line of the hull. For example, the large steamer *Jacob Strader*, built in 1853 for the Mail Line, and a predecessor of the *United States* and the *America*, had a hull only 27.5 feet wide, but when measured over the guards her main deck was 69 feet across! The *Strader* was an extreme case, but it was common for guards to make the main deck 50 to 75 per cent wider than the hull. Guards also gave extra storage space for freight and fuel and provided a place for passengers to promenade.

Guards could make the steamboat dangerously unstable, and with the type of boilers in use on western boats at the time, a list of even ten or twelve inches to one side could cause the boilers to malfunction, which, if prolonged, could result in an explosion. This made it dangerous, for example, when passengers would crowd to one side of a boat to observe an attraction.

Even at that, of those passengers who escaped to the guards of the *United States* many had not time to jump into the river. Some people wandered about in a daze, as others rushed headlong into the flames! One passenger on the *United States* said the progress of the fire from the bow of the boat to her stern was about as fast as a man could walk.

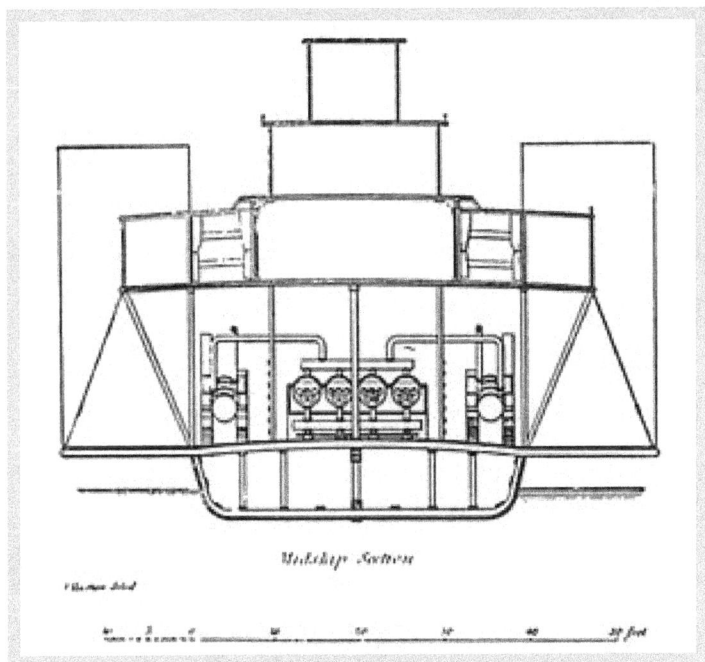

Diagram of common steamboat guards (from Wikipedia).

As the *America* backed away from the blazing *United States*, the latter boat was also trying to get in to the Indiana shore, but the *America* was blocking her. This caused the *United States* to drift downstream broadside to the current and the two boats came together a second time and lay side by side, both headed upstream, as the *United States* sank in shallow water. Passengers and crew of the *United States* began jumping down to the lower deck of the *America*, a distance of at least fifteen feet, but the fire had now spread to the river side of the forward cabin of the *America*, as well. The *America's* crew fought valiantly to put out the fire, but the force of the wind soon had the fire raging all over the upper works.

On the *America*, Captain David Whitten, standing on the hurricane deck (the roof of the Texas), observed the plight of the passengers and crew of the stricken *United States*. He disregarded danger to his own boat, passengers, and crew, and told Pilot Jenkins to steer her again to the side of her sister boat, where he attempted to hold her. Flames leapt over to her from the *United States*, but Whitten's heroic action saved many lives, even though it caused the total loss of the *America*.

The *America's* engines had backed for over a minute prior to the collision and they continued backing for some time afterward. The great wheels of both steamers had wildly thrashed the water in reverse, but they collided before the momentum of either boat could be overcome. When the collision occurred, the sister boats were about 100 yards below Rayl's Landing. The *America's* engines continued working until the boat was made fast to the Indiana shore.

But for the presence of the many barrels of flammable liquids at the very point of impact, fire would not have resulted and there would likely have been few fatalities. Captain Charles Wade of the *United States* later said that were it not for the fire, he could have run his boat ashore and saved almost everything. About the time the fire spread to the forecastle of the *America*, the burning liquids ran off the deck of the *United States*. Soon the surface of the river was covered with a sheet of flame.

Pilot Napoleon Jenkins, the engineer James Holmes, and the clerk W. T. Taylor, all of the *America*, distinguished themselves in the minutes after the collision. Many passengers on the *America* owed their lives to one or more of this heroic trio. Taylor saved the actual passenger list, not just the list of people who bought tickets, which later allowed an accounting that revealed only four persons had perished on the *America*. He then went through the cabin breaking open doors of the staterooms and helping passengers escape. Jenkins stood at his wheel while the hissing, crackling flames closed around him. James Holmes, too, stayed at his post in the engine room until the very last when Jenkins rang him off (released him from duty). Only when the *America* was secure against the Indiana shore did Jenkins and Holmes leave their posts to avoid suffocation and make their way to safety.

Another brave spirit was the third clerk of the United States, James Johns, 23, of Louisville. In the *Cincinnati Enquirer* of December 6th, it was reported that until the last moment before he was driven by the flames to abandon his work, he provided several ladies and children of the doomed vessel with life preservers. Just before he leapt into the river he was heard to say that he could not swim, but by that time there was no helping hand left to save the young hero.

Sadly, an account in the *Cincinnati Gazette* dated December 9th stated, "The body of James W. Johns, receiving clerk on the *United States*, was recovered. It is said he was the last man to leave the boat. He kept with the ladies, placing life preservers around them until the vessel was ready to sink. After working to the last moment to save the lives of others, he found it too late to save himself. He perished in the flames of the burning oil on the surface of the water. Mr. Johns died a hero." He was rightly honored for his work saving others, but his passenger register was destroyed in the fire.

Passengers' Peril

On December 26, 1868, *Harper's Weekly* published this illustration by E.P. Frazer of the collision between the *United States* and the *America*.

☙

Ole Bull, on the *America*, had retired to his stateroom when the crash came. With the others, he hurried out, but then remembered his precious violin he'd left behind. He threw off friendly hands which tried to prevent him from returning to his room, groped through the suffocating smoke, retrieved the beloved instrument that meant more than life to the old maestro and staggered out onto the guard. Nearly blind from the smoke, he stumbled over a coil of rope on the deck and fell into the river clutching his violin. Somehow he landed on his feet where the water was little more than waist deep and free of fire. Holding the instrument above his head, he was dragged by one of the *America's* crew to the muddy bank, his violin remaining almost completely dry. His instrument had been saved, but Maestro Bull lost his concert clothes, money, and valuables, including a golden laurel wreath the Masons in New York had given him.

The others in Bull's troupe survived as well, including his soloist, Miss Barton, whose room had to be broken into and its occupant rescued by force. Not until she was safe on dry land did she realize the gravity of the situation.

Meanwhile, on the *United States*, Oliver Noble, the mate, was awakened in his room in the Texas where he slept with his little son, Lon. From the signals exchanged between the boats, it seemed to him there was soon to be trouble. The bell cords from the pilot house to the engine room ran along just under the ceiling in Oliver Noble's room, and the rapid jerking of the cords slapping against the ceiling alarmed him. He jumped into his clothes and ran down to the forecastle. In an instant he saw that to remain where he was would mean certain death, and that one or both boats would be sunk. He rushed back up to the Texas to awaken and save his boy.

He took his little boy downstairs, and was preparing to jump overboard with him from the stern of the *United States* when a lady rushed up begging him to save her. He told her to jump in the river ahead of him and he would do his best to get her to shore. She was afraid to jump so Oliver took her in his strong arms and threw her overboard. He then grabbed Lon and followed with the boy in his arms. Oliver was a powerful man and an expert swimmer. He got hold of the lady and made it to shore with both her and the boy.

A Mr. W.W. Hanley, a passenger on the United States from Cincinnati, remembered seeing the barrels of coal oil stowed on the forecastle, so he went downstairs to the lower deck near the stern and jumped in the river. He was singed by the flames on the water, which made swimming in the cold muddy river a terrible ordeal. He saw several people who were burned much worse than he carried away by the current into the darkness.

A large yawl (lifeboat) overloaded with passengers passed Mr. Hanley, going downstream. They turned and started in toward shore, but the *America* came backing down and they were caught under her wheel buckets, crushing the boat and its occupants.

He saw another yawl hanging from the boom at the stern of the *United States*. After helping others till the last minute, the deckhands started crawling out on the boom one by one and lowering themselves into the yawl, which was swinging back and forth. Too many men tried to get into the boat, and, as they lowered it into the water, one of the supporting ropes snapped, plunging the men into the water where, it was later learned, sixteen of the twenty drowned. The painter (rope) on the bow end of the yawl did not break, and the lifeboat was left swinging in a vertical position, empty.

On the *United States*, among those who lingered in the ballroom when the captain stopped the celebration were Eva Jones and her mother, who were enjoying a conversation with Eva's new friend, Mary Johnson. Joe McCammant went to his stateroom.

Marcus Toney decided to take some air at the stern rail before retiring. He watched as the *United States* dropped down around the sharp bend past the mouth of Sugar Creek, then crossed over from the Kentucky side and lined up in the straight stretch of channel that ran down the Indiana side to Rayl's Landing.

For Marcus Toney that night the name of his boat, the *United States*, and her sister, the *America*, represented an irony for the Confederate veteran from Nashville, Tennessee. He was also a former inmate at the draconian Union Army prison at Elmira, New York. The fact that Mr. Toney now worked for the New York Central Railroad continued his unlikely association with the Empire State, and doubled the irony. He also found that as a Confederate veteran he couldn't vote or buy government land under the Homestead Act, but all the while he had to pay taxes.

Mr. Toney escaped death again on this night, as he had done countless times during the war. After the collision and the resulting inferno, he scrambled through the smoke and confusion, returning to his room to claim his watch and money. He then crawled some 200 feet along the deck beneath the smothering smoke toward the stern. He said later, "Mothers were shrieking for husbands and children, husbands calling for wives. In all my privations in life, I have never witnessed such a heart-rending scene, but it was all I could do to save myself." He tried to jump onto the *America* before she pulled away in the confusion, but he was prevented by the flames. His battle instincts proved worthy, for when the *America* finally came near a second time, Toney leaped from the flaming boat, plummeting more than a dozen feet to the deck of the *America*. He was severely injured, and might have died had a man not carried him on his back to shore. He heard someone say later that 130 passengers on the *United States* went down – what would have been a good week's work for the Reaper at Elmira Prison.

After being rescued and receiving the best care from his brothers in the Masonic Lodge at Warsaw, Toney was taken to Louisville on the *General Lytle*. Although suffering acutely, he was able to leave for home on the cars of the *L & N*, one of the earliest and most successful railroads in the region, chartered in 1850.

Among the many stories of heroism in the course of the disaster, there were a few tales of the dark side of human nature. The *Madison Courier* of December 8th contained this account: "A gentleman and his sister, a lovely young lady, were passengers on the *United States*. At the first shock he was thrown from his bed. He dressed and rushed to the stateroom of his sister, burst open the door, seized her in his arms and carried her down to the main deck. There he procured a door shutter and threw it overboard and leaped after it with his sister still in his arms. He placed her securely on the shutter and was pushing it with its precious burden toward the shore when to his horror a large able-bodied man swam up and pushed the sister off the board and climbed on it himself. The girl sank with a scream, and if she came to the surface it was so dark that her brother could not find her. The brother, maddened by the dastardly act, made after the man, and seizing him by the throat, engaged him in a fight to the death. The brother survived to tell the tragic story, but the sister was lost."

As for Miss Mary Johnson of Madison, it was announced in the *Louisville Courier Journal* that the day following the disaster at the Madison shipyards the body of a young woman, with a life-preserver attached, was found floating in the river. In her belt was found a paper with the name Eva Jones on it, and it was first assumed the body was she. Afterward, the body was recognized as that of Mary Johnson. It was possible to identify her because she had drowned and not burned. She had thus come back to the father who so anxiously awaited her return from her extended trip. But, instead of a welcoming celebration there was a funeral.

A surviving passenger on the *United States* said that Mary's cousin Lewis, after vainly trying to find Mary after the collision, leaped from the flaming boat when at too great a distance to make the shore, and was lost.

The Reverend Lucien Rule, of Goshen, Kentucky, in a September 1, 1929, letter to the *Courier Journal*, told the following story:

"During the earlier celebration in honor of the two wedding parties on board the *United States*, the lovely young ladies, Mary Johnson and Eva Jones, had been introduced to each other by Mr. J. N. Price. He gave to each of these charming girls the address of the other, which they stuck in their belts. The merry laughter and song had just subsided when the crash came. In the ensuing panic, Miss Jones rushed to Mr. Price, asking him to save her, but with sorrow he replied that he must give his attention first to his wife and children.

"When Joe McCammant rushed from his stateroom and found Nellie Jones and her daughter Eva after the collision, both were hysterical. They clung to their escort screaming. With difficulty he freed himself and got them out on the guard. He finally calmed Eva enough to get a life preserver on her and hand her a shutter. She then moved away from him so that he could try and save her mother. He got Nellie as far as the railing, and tried to get her to jump in the river so that he could follow and try to get her ashore. He had her part of the way up on the railing when she suddenly became hysterical again and jumped to the floor. She tore loose from him and ran back toward the flames. He followed and caught her, picked her up in his arms and carried her back. He lifted her almost to the top of the rail, ready to heave her over, but she fought him like a trapped wild animal. While they struggled, his clothing caught fire and spread rapidly. This became so painful he could not bear it. He sprang over the railing and into the river just barely in time to save his own life.

"The water put out the fire on his clothing, but the pain from his burns was excruciating. He tried to swim but both his legs cramped until they were useless to keep him afloat. He was starting to go down when a familiar voice near him called, 'Is that you, Joe?' It was Captain Richard Wade. He caught his friend and kept him from going down. The captain had two planks, and he helped Joe onto one of them and started paddling him to shore. But other people jumping into the river from the guards above separated the two men.

"McCammant paddled weakly on downstream, desperately trying not to lose consciousness. He reached shore somewhere farther down river, and by a miracle got his face and one arm out on the muddy shore before he passed out. Some men watching from the riverbank above ran down to the water's edge, pulled him out, and carried him to a nearby farmhouse.

"Meanwhile, Eva Jones had run out onto the guard. Just a short time before she had been surrounded by young men seeking to dance with her, but now when the boat was sinking in flames she sought some man to help save her life.

"Just at that time a young man and his wife came hurrying out upon the guard. He was the son of a retired minister. When they left home, the boy's father came to the river with them to see them off. As they parted, the father asked them to promise him that in case they were in any danger, they would pause and pray and ask for Divine guidance before they made any move. They promised to do so.

"This night, as other passengers ran screaming from their rooms, this young couple knelt for a moment beside their stateroom bed and said a prayer, then rose and began to seek safety. As they came out on the guard, Eva Jones ran to them begging them to help her. She pleaded, 'Save me! Save me! I know I'm a little rebel, but I need help.' " Earlier, she must have made no secret of her Southern sympathies.

"She put her hand on the young man's arm and her eyes were full of tears. Her voice was choking and it seemed that she was almost addressing a prayer to him. A look of pain came into the boy's eyes. He paused to look at her, then at his wife. She pulled at her husband and gave him a look as if she thought he was endangering their own lives and wasting time. The young man hesitated just a brief moment looking at Eva, then pulled his arm free. He told her to watch for an opportunity, then jump in the river." And so, for the third time in those desperate moments, a man turned to save others and left Eva Jones alone.

"The young couple hurried on down the guard aft of the port side wheel. Eva looked after them briefly, then prepared to take the young man's advice. As she started to jump, had a protective friend been there, her life might have been saved, but there was no watchful person to warn her that she was jumping into the path of the *America's* approaching starboard wheel.

"The *America* came alongside and banged into the *United States*. The young man and his wife climbed up on the railing and jumped the fifteen feet down to the guard of the *America*. Neither was seriously injured. The *America* backed down along the Indiana shore, and when she managed to land, the young couple was waiting on the guard next to the bank, the side of the boat mostly free of fire at that moment. When the boat touched they jumped ashore. They climbed to the top of the bank and walked upstream above the *America* and could see both boats burning. The flames lit up the surface of the river, its water filled with screaming passengers and crew struggling to keep afloat. Many cries of agony went up from those whose oil-soaked clothing was burning the life from them.

"If the young couple had let Eva walk down the guard with them she might now be standing beside them on the riverbank, but they never learned her fate." No one said a prayer for Eva, and there had been no brave and strong Oliver Noble at her side.

Reverend Rule's letter continued: "When the U. S. Mail Line's steamer *C. T. Dumont* arrived at the scene from Cincinnati under orders of the company president, Mr. Pearce, all the Cincinnati victims who were able to be moved were put aboard and taken home. Captain Richard Wade had Joe McCammant put on board, and went with him to supervise his care.

"Captain John Scott and his wife placed Joe McCammant, who was badly burned about the back, face, and neck, in their own home under the care of nurses until he recovered. He was inconsolable over his failure to save the Jones ladies from the inferno on the *United States*. Then Mr. Scott and his wife made the trip down the river seeking information as to the fate of Nellie and Eva Jones. At the scene, someone gave the Scotts a ring they believed to be Nellie's. They heard the story of Eva being crushed by the *America's* wheel."

In those days there were two steamboat landings in Vevay, Indiana, the Lower Grade and the Upper Grade. The wharfboat used by steamers lay at the Lower Grade. A large float for mooring and unloading coal barges was located at the Upper Grade at the foot of Washington Street. The Upper Grade was a favorite spot for retired river men to gather on summer evenings and swap yarns. Fishermen kept their boats there, and they brought their nets there to dry.

More than four months after the great disaster, on a warm and balmy day, a group of old timers sat on a bench at the top of the riverbank. The collision was still the most popular topic of conversation, but it was the general opinion that all the bodies that would ever appear had already been found.

Some boys ran up to where the old men were sitting and shouted that a woman's body had just floated in to shore. Townspeople gathered, but the coroner was out of town. John Clendening was Justice of the Peace, and he was the designated alternate coroner. John called on Constable Vincent Bright to subpoena six jurors to hold an inquest over the body of the woman. They later signed the report, which identified the woman as Eva Jones, 20 to 25 years old. The detailed description of her fine clothing revealed her name embroidered on the band of her underwear. The jury declared that she died by drowning and was one of the victims of the collision at Rayl's Landing on December 4, 1868.

The Vevay *Reveille-Enterprise* on May 20, 1869, reported, "The body of a young lady was found in the river near Vevay by Orlando Rouse. She was identified as Miss Eva Jones, of Florida, a victim of the *United States* and *America* disaster." The report concluded with the words, "The remains were sent to friends." To some, the friendship of these two lovely girls and their tragic deaths was the saddest incident of the whole tragedy.

Also in the summer of 1869, a report was published in the *Vevay Democrat* of bills paid to T. D. Wright and sons for inquests appearing in the paper. Of the 34 inquests listed, six of them, including Eva Jones, were directly attributed to the steamboat collision. This list, plus the 54 compiled by Mr. Tait at Rayl's Landing in the days following the collision (see list at the end of this book), puts the total number of known victims at 60, but this is undoubtedly far short of the actual number of fatalities. For example, President Pearce of the Mail Line appointed Frank Carter, a company director and manager of the company office and wharf at Louisville, to come up to the wreck site and take charge of salvage operations and the search for bodies. Frank and his assistant, Andrew Harrington, the freight clerk from the *United States*, made their headquarters at Warsaw. Later, the *Cincinnati Commercial* published the following notice: "Thirty-three bodies recovered from the wrecks and from the water. Frank Carter, in charge of salvage." It is not known if this list overlapped the one provided by coroner Tait following the disaster. For some time following the collision, bodies like those of Mary Johnson and Eva Jones were discovered at various locations downriver from the wreck, and the number of bodies lost in the river will forever be unknown. Statements of the number of fatalities from the disaster ranged from 40 to 170, perhaps the most likely estimate being 74.

Angels of Mercy

Lee Cohn, of Cincinnati, a passenger on the *United States*, said, "I came out of my stateroom and found flames all around me. I threw my coat onto the *America* as she drifted past us, then realized to save my life I would have to swim. I slid down a post to the lower deck, and there took off my boots and threw them in the river. I waited until a floating mass of burning wood passed me and then saw that the river was filled with people. I could see their heads and didn't want to jump on them, so I waited until the left side of my face was licked by the flames. I could remain no longer, so I jumped in the river and swam to shore. I saw no one escape from the boat after I left.

"On shore, I saw by the light of the fire a farmhouse in the distance. I finally reached this house barefooted and coatless and found the owners giving clothing and assistance to the large number of people who had found their way there." This farmhouse was the residence of Elias Rayl and his family.

Among the first to arrive at the top of the riverbank at Rayl's Landing after the collision were Elias Rayl and his wife and daughter, who had been awakened by the crash. Their home was closer to the landing than any other residence, a short distance back from the top of the riverbank. The Rayls were stunned for a moment until they saw people coming up the riverbank carrying the injured.

Mrs. Rayl and her daughter took charge, and with Eli's assistance they led the slow procession to their house. The Rayls filled their beds with sufferers, then emptied their closets of quilts and blankets to make pallets on the floor. Mrs. Rayl tore up sheets and pillow cases for bandages. When her supplies were exhausted, she sent men on horseback scouring the neighborhood to borrow more. She assisted doctors when they arrived, bathed wounds, and applied soothing liniments and bandages. The Rayl home soon became a hospital, and many lives were saved, but as the night wore on, the house became for some a chamber of death.

The Rayls gladly stripped their house of anything that would be conducive to the comfort of those who made their escape from the burning wrecks. Other families within reach of the sufferers deprived themselves in the same manner.

When the Rayl house could hold no more, groups of men carried more victims to neighboring houses farther from the landing. John Fothergill searched among the survivors and found a dozen half-drowned men, many of them elderly, and helped revive them until they were able to follow him on foot to his home. There he warmed them before his fireplace, helped them remove their wet clothing, dressed them from his not-too-plentiful supply of clothes, and gave them food and coffee.

Captain Nichols was among Fothergill's guests, and he later described his host as one of the kindest and least selfish men he had ever met. The *Cincinnati Gazette*, on December 7th stated, "Charles Nichols, of Covington, a pilot on the *Minnie*, had taken sick at Louisville and was returning home on the *America*. He was in the pilot house talking with Neb

Jenkins, and when the steamer was near the wreck of the *Thomas Scott* along the Kentucky shore, just above Warsaw, he understood from the exchange of whistles that a collision was inevitable. He rushed to his room, got his overcoat, and was on the main deck when the crash came. He got safely to shore, and when he reached the Rayl's farmhouse he could hear the bells ringing in Warsaw. Later he was interviewed and said, 'The Rayl family treated me and the others mighty kindly. I was taken to the Fothergills' farmhouse later, where with ten other men I spent the rest of the night. This family furnished all of us with clothing and wouldn't charge a cent. Other survivors were given shelter at houses above the Fothergills'.'"

On December 9th, a map of the area of the collision was published in the *Cincinnati Daily Gazette*. It was drawn by Ashton Craig of Warsaw who was clerk on the *C. T. Dumont*, one of the rescue boats. It shows the locations of other nearby Indiana families near Rayl's Landing with the names Fothergill, Snyder, Hickman, Woods, Campbell, and Harris.

When daylight came up slowly on Saturday morning, December 5th, the *America* did not arrive on time at the Mail Line wharfboat at Cincinnati. The morning wore on and still the big steamer did not appear.

At 9:30 AM a telegraph dispatch was received from the company president, Christopher G. Pearce, from Warsaw, Kentucky, stating the bare facts of the disaster, and that 100 lives were believed to have been lost.

The message included orders that the Mail Line steamer *C. T. Dumont* be sent from Cincinnati to the scene of the accident. The *Dumont* departed at once for Rayl's Landing.

Little additional information followed for an agonizing period of time. There were no telephones, except along the railroad lines, which were at a great distance from the accident scene, and telegraph offices were very few. Existing roads were too narrow for anything much larger than riders on horseback, and they were rough and uneven in summer and quagmires in winter. River boats themselves were the fastest means of communication at that time.

In Cincinnati, the bulletin board of the *Cincinnati Gazette* was surrounded all day by relatives and friends of passengers who had left Friday night or were expected Saturday morning. Saturday, Sunday and Monday were gloomy days in Cincinnati.

On Sunday, December 6th, the steamer *S.B. Graham* came up from Madison to pick up the injured from the Rayls' and other homes, and the bodies of those identified as Madison residents.

On Monday it was announced that the steamer *C.T. Dumont* was due back in Cincinnati at 8 PM with survivors and some of the dead. Long before the appointed hour, a large crowd had gathered at the wharf in the raw and chilly weather. Then news came that the *Dumont* would be delayed until 11 PM. The crowd thinned, and many of the people went up the hill, but most had returned before 11 PM.

It was a solemn group of people, and even the sparse conversation was conducted in low tones. A young man who had applied for a clerk's job on the

United States on her last departure, and had almost been accepted, whispered to a friend how grateful he was to have been turned down. One lady on the wharf rushed to the river to board the *United States* as a passenger and had arrived too late. She got there just in time to see the boat rounding to, disappearing into the darkness on her last voyage. The lady was angry then, but tonight she was in a mood of quiet thanksgiving as she waited on the wharf.

It was almost midnight when from the darkness down the river came the long low whistle of the *C.T. Dumont*. Then the dim lights of her kerosene lamps became visible. The wharfboat doors opened, admitting the piercing wind, while in the hearts of those waiting hope was mixed with dread.

The people crowded to the edge of the wharfboat guards, heedless of danger. The rousters tried unsuccessfully to hold them back. The timbers of the wharfboat creaked as swells from the wheels rushed under the wharf.

Someone on the boiler deck of the boat called, "Oh, Jim, Jim!" as the *Dumont* approached, and Jim on the wharf gave one great shout, but could say no more, for he was weeping like a child. The crew could hardly make the boat fast for the crowd surging on board and up the forward stairway.

What a scene! Joyous reunion with survivors, heartbreak for those who found their dead from the tiers of those who had drowned or whose remains were charred by the fire, and the despair of those whose loved ones were not there.

The town of Warsaw also witnessed the suffering, heartbreak, and hope of many. Quoting from the *Madison Courier* of December 8th, "The scene at Warsaw beggars description: relatives searching for each other, the injured screaming with pain, ladies having perforce to go to bed while their linen was being dried. Clothing was brought by the open-handed and warm-hearted citizens of Warsaw, and everything was done to make them as comfortable as possible under the circumstances, including medical care by Dr. Baxter, of Warsaw." People here in the Border Country along the Ohio, often divided by loyalties to opposing sides in the Civil War, now worked shoulder to shoulder with their neighbors in serving the needs of these helpless victims of the disaster.

Ole Bull, having arrived safely at Warsaw, conceived the idea of playing his violin to raise the morale of the still dazed and grief-stricken survivors. He and his troupe, all having survived the wreck, arranged to give a concert. The lobby of the Lindell Hotel was packed with an attentive crowd, and it was said that never before or since has such beautiful music been heard in Warsaw. Maestro Bull was a world renowned musician. A former child prodigy, he was admitted to the Bergen, Norway, orchestra as first violin at the age of eight.

Col. J.S. Golladay, a Kentucky Congressman, reported, "I was a passenger on the *America*, and was asleep when the collision occurred. Awakened by the impact and sounds of running footsteps, I looked out the window to see fire spreading across the water. I dressed hurriedly, but calmly, secured my watch, my pocketbook, and shawl and went out the door onto the guard to find the *United States* sunk and the cabin a solid wall of flames. The *America* was also on fire at one end and on the side next to the river. I found a throng of people running to and fro, screaming and praying. Now and then one or two of them jumped into the river as the boat was receding from the shore. Unable to swim, I hesitated to take to the water, but went to the edge to jump. Encouraged by a Negro on the shore, I took the dreaded leap and was assisted to the shore by the same Negro. The *Lady Grace* appeared at the scene soon after, and I was taken aboard for the trip over to Warsaw, where I found some of my wife's people, Mr. Brown and family, who treated me very kindly. The next night I took the *Lytle* up to Cincinnati."

The towboat *Reindeer* had come up the river from Warsaw a few minutes after the collision and rendered considerable help in rescuing passengers from the burning steamers. The Cincinnati and Madison packet *Lady Grace*, which was downbound, arrived at the scene about an hour after the accident. She took on board Golladay and other survivors who had taken shelter at the Rayl residence and their neighbors' houses, and conveyed most of them to Warsaw in two trips, and took some on to Madison.

On December 8th the *Cincinnati Commercial* quoted Captain R.H. Woolfolk, of Louisville. "The people of Warsaw gave themselves up wholly to the alleviation of the distressed. Every man, woman, and child in the town exerted themselves unceasingly as long as there was one poor unfortunate in need of succor."

After the boats had sunk and burned, some of their officers spent the entire night around the scene. It must have been a heavy-hearted group that stood on the river bank when daylight finally came. At noon the next day, Charles Marshall, the engineer on watch on the *United States*, was still down by the river in his wet clothing. In the morning, nothing of the wreck was visible but a few charred timbers sticking up out of the water, and corpses being laid in rows along the shore.

A dispatch dated December 6th was sent from Madison to the *Cincinnati Gazette*. "The steamer *J.L. Graham* will leave at two today for the wreck, taking seven skiffs, 20 men, two days' rations, with drags and nets to search for bodies. A six-pounder cannon goes along with the party, which will be fired on the bank in the hope of raising bodies."

The *Commercial* of December 16th had this macabre news comment: "The bodies recovered from the sunken *United States* for identification were ranged alongside each other on the river bank and were in a remarkable state of preservation because of the cold weather. Parties were arriving hourly to identify their friends and loved ones, but many went away with sinking hearts, for the charred corpses bore little resemblance to those they knew."

There were doubtless several coroners' inquests over the bodies of the victims as they were discovered at various locations downriver from the accident. The inquest report at the end of this book, conducted at Rayl's Landing, may have been the largest.

On December 8th the salvage vessel, *Champion*, was sent from Louisville to the scene of the wrecks, but she failed to raise the sunken *United States*. Then on December 12th the *Underwriter* arrived on the scene from Cairo. The *Cincinnati Commercial* said of the *Underwriter*: "The impression prevails that owing to her extensive rigging, pumps and wrecking facilities she will succeed in raising the *United States*." Then on the 18th the same newspaper said, "The hull of the ill-fated *United States* has been raised by the submarine (as salvage vessels were then called) *Underwriter*. The charred hull with her wheelhouse standing will be towed here for repairs. Her bow was almost completely cut off. The hull will have to be towed here stern foremost." Another news item said, "The wreck of the *United States* arrived here in tow of the towboat *Coal Hill* and the submarine *Underwriter*."

Captain Eckert of the *Underwriter* completed the raising of the remains of the *United States* using the equipment she had on board, as well as the floating equipment. The wreck was supported by barges alongside to hold her up, and was towed back to Cincinnati. Some of the freight on the *United States* was salvaged, and an auction was conducted by Walter Ezekiel where the boat was moored at the foot of Vine

Street. The *United States* was then towed up to Cincinnati Marine Ways where she was eventually rebuilt and put back in service, with Charles Dufour as captain. The wreck of the *America* still lies in the mud on the river bottom near Rayl's Landing.

Aftermath

The loss of the two state of the art Mail Line boats left the company without enough boats to carry on its business. On the day following the disaster, T.G. Gaylord, of David Gibson and Company, offered them the use of their boat, the *St. Charles*. The offer was accepted and the entire crew of the *America* was placed on the *St. Charles*, except Napoleon Jenkins. In Jenkins's place, Captain Charles Dufour returned to his regular duties and was placed on the *St. Charles* as pilot. Several other boats had their itineraries changed to meet the needs of the Mail Line Company.

The Board of Steamboat Inspectors convened at Cincinnati almost immediately after the disaster to investigate the tragic accident. After interviewing many surviving passengers, officers, and crew of the two ill-fated steamers, they published their findings on February 15, 1869, in a ten-page Official Report.

Many accounts of the incident have appeared in print over the years since it happened, but author Dr.

Carl Bogardus, of Warsaw, Kentucky, who wrote *Glimpses Into The Past On The Ohio River* in 1977-1980, considered the Inspectors' Report to be the most accurate description of the tragedy and its causes up to that time.

In 1868, three documents were required of each steamboat in service on the Ohio River: the Enrollment Document, the Inspectors' Certificate and the License of a vessel above 20 tons. During the investigation of the accident, all three documents were produced by the company for each boat, and they were up to date. These documents had been mandated by the Steamboat Inspection Service that was created by an Act of Congress in July, 1838. The law provided for an "Annual inspection of hulls, boilers, machinery and general equipment of vessels subject to steamboat inspection laws." Unfortunately, the law did not provide for enforcement, or fines for violations. In any event, the two boats involved in the Rayl's Landing tragedy appeared to be in compliance with the law, and the accident was not blamed on faulty equipment.

At least some of the litigation arising from the accident was conducted at Vevay, Indiana, the county seat of Switzerland County, on whose shore the wrecked vessels came to rest. At the time of this writing the originals of the three required documents for both the *United States* and the *America* are on display at the "Life on the Ohio" River History Museum in Vevay, Indiana. The documents may have been inadvertently left at Vevay after the lawsuits were concluded.

Most newspaper accounts of the collision placed all the blame on Pilot Jenkins's head and none on Remlein, but the report of Steamboat Inspectors H.H. Devenny and C.W. Fisher stated otherwise. "Mr. Remlein, pilot of the *United States*, violated the requirement of Rule One in that he signaled before hearing that of the ascending boat, which we consider the prime cause of the collision."

Among the principal findings of the Report were: "After a careful review of the testimony it is the opinion of the Board that the pilots on both boats were at fault. The pilot of the *America*, when he first signaled, blew two sounds of the whistle, and while sounding the first blast, that of the *United States* was evidently also blown, one sound simultaneously, and ceasing with the first sound of the *America's* whistle, which entirely prevented the pilot of the *United States* from hearing it. Hearing only the second sound blown at that time by the *America*, he came ahead."

The Report went on to state, "Mr. Jenkins, pilot of the *America*, admits hearing but one whistle in answer to the whistles blown by him . . . he also continued to come ahead after the whistles were exchanged (and before he ordered engines reversed)... at which time the two boats were but 400 yards apart. This was a clear violation of Rule Two, which states that if the signals are not received and understood by the time the boats are 800 yards apart, both pilots must stop until the whistles are understood before proceeding. Jenkins then should have stopped the engines and checked his headway until the proper signals were given and understood."

The law did empower the inspectors to suspend licenses of pilots in cases where they were found negligent. The Inspectors, H.H. Devenny and C.W. Fisher, concluded their report by stating, "Both pilots were experienced and were also skilled in their profession, but in this case the collision could have been avoided . . . and because of their failure to abide by the rules . . . we hereby revoke the licenses of Jacob Remlein and Napoleon B. Jenkins to act as pilots of steamboats from the date hereof."

The U.S. Mail Line Company made an effort to reimburse passengers and crew members for their losses, compensated those "Good Samaritans" who aided the victims, paid medical and burial bills, and covered the costs for Coroners' Inquests. Many lawsuits were filed against the company, but only in Indiana courts. The cases dragged on for many years, and just when matters seemed settled by offers from the company, the question arose as to where the accident actually occurred, Indiana or Kentucky. Earlier rulings had supported Kentucky's claim that its territory extended to the shoreline on the Indiana side of the river. This caused the whole affair to be thrown out of the courts.

There were also loud complaints from the participants in the litigation that H.H. Devenny, one of the two inspectors in the case, had never served in any operational role on a steamboat, and was thus unqualified to rule in the case.

Historical Perspective

In 1875, James Stewart bought the Indiana farm bordering on Bryant's Creek and the Ohio River, the former Rayl farm. Tenants on his farm were an African-American family. The old grandmother once said, shaking her head solemnly and pointing to the scene of the steamboat disaster, "I never look over that way after dark!" One day her grandson was down on the bank of the river poking around for shells when he unearthed the case of a small gold watch. Inside the lid was engraved "Dora Cook." This find came to the notice of the editor of the *Vevay Reveille*, W.J. Baird, and he printed a story about it, adding questions as to who Dora Cook might have been. Other papers copied the story and presently letters came from a Mrs. Cook and a Mr. McFerrin, of St. Louis. It was their daughter and son, respectively, who were the younger of the bridal couples on board the *United States*, and neither survived. On identification, the watch case was sent to Mrs. Cook and the finder was suitably rewarded.

The following article was brought to light in the publication *Northern Kentucky Views* around 2015. It was apparently found in a newspaper printed in a community near the site of the wreck. From the statement that the lamp had been in the water 27 years after the 1868 collision, the newspaper clipping probably dated from 1895.

"During the low water and the pleasant weather of the past couple of weeks there have been quite a number of visitors to the wreck of the steamer *America*, which lies at the mouth of Bryant's Creek. The double-cabined steamers *America* and *United States* collided about Bryant's Creek the night of December 4, 1868.

"Both parts of the ill-fated (*America*) are plain to be seen now, and nearly every day parties go there to dig for relics, and usually get something of value. (For example,) several silver strainer spoons used in the bar (were found). The lamp (that was found) was half-filled with coal oil, and although it had been in the water twenty-seven years, it is still in serviceable condition. Several other articles of value were found and all were in good condition. There was quite a large crowd at the wreck Sunday afternoon, Vevay, Florence, Markland, and Warsaw being well represented. The hulk is covered with mud and drift and everything of value is obtained by digging or dragging in the water."

In 1934, Mrs. Belle Summons Brown, a septuagenarian living at Warsaw, vividly remembered that as a child of ten she and her family saw the two burning steamers from the upstairs window of their house, two miles above Warsaw. She said to her father, William Summons, "It's the Aurora Borealis." Her father said, "Aurora Borealis, hell, it's a steamboat fire!" In three-quarters of an hour it was over. Both boats had burned to the waterline and all survivors were on the Indiana shore. The conflagration had lighted the sky, visible for miles around, and now it had receded to darkness again.

Mr. James Stewart told a visitor to his farm in the 1940s that in order to show their appreciation for the help rendered the survivors of the tragedy by Elias Rayl and his family, the U.S. Mail Line gave them passes good for any time and any place on their boats. At that time in the 1940s no one named Rayl lived on or near their original farm.

In the 1950s, Robert McCann, purser on the steamer *Delta Queen*, told a passenger that following the disaster, the U.S. Mail Line, to further show their appreciation for the kindnesses of the Rayl family, had their ship's carpenters build the Rayls a new house. This house was damaged by the 1937 flood and the porch torn away, but it stood until 1954. The U.S. Mail Line spelled the name "Rail," and Elias Rayl said, "If the company wants it that way, then that's the way it will be." The navigation charts continued showing that location, until at least the 1970s, as "Rails Landing Light."

The losses to all parties were great. The company lost two of its finest steamers, and the insurance payments were far from enough to replace them. Still, the company was in sound financial condition and continued rendering service between Cincinnati and Louisville until the Great Depression forced it out of business in 1931.

APPENDIX

From the *Vevay Reveille*
Vol. 52, No. 2, Jan. 1869, P. 2, Col. 5:

NOTICE

Is hereby given that an inquest was held by me at Rayl's Landing, Switzerland County, Indiana, on December the 6th and 15th, inclusive, A.D. 1868, over the following described bodies.

The verdict of the several juries in these cases was that the described persons, No. 1 and No. 54, inclusive, came to their death by and because of the burning and sinking of the steamers *United States* and *America*, occasioned by the colliding of said steamers at Rayl's Landing in York Township, Switzerland County, State of Indiana.

Witness my hand and seal this 15th day of December, A.D. 1868

JAMES TAIT (seal)

Coroner of Switzerland County, Indiana

Published Jan. 7, 1869

No. 1. Unknown body; about 20 years of age, medium size; had 1 gold ring on third finger left hand; 1 diamond ring on same finger; 2 diamond rings on 1st and 2d fingers of same hand; 1 anchor ring on 3rd finger right hand; 1 jet bracelet on each arm; 1 black glass ear ring.

No. 2. Female child, about 10 years of age.

No. 3. Unknown body, badly burned; found on her breast 1 ring marked "M."

No. 4. Unknown man; about 20 years of age; about 5 feet 5 inches in height; badly burned.

No. 5. Unknown man; medium size; piece of farmer's satin coat being found on arm; badly burned.

No. 6. Unknown lady, badly burned.

No. 7. Unknown lady, badly burned.

No. 8. Unknown man; about 45 years of age; 5 feet 10 inches in height, badly burned.

No. 9. Emile Moran; age 35 years; had on person 1 comb, 1 letter, 1 silver watch with guard and gold drop; 5 keys; 1 knife; 1 gold breast pin; cash $45.65.

No. 10. Body of John Fannell, Covington, Ky.; age 49 years

No. 11. James W. John, 3d clerk steamer U. S.; age 23 years.

No. 12. Wallace Ferris; age 45 years; 1 gold ring on his person.

No. 13. William Johnson; age 26 years; height 5 feet; had on black coat and pants and stoga boots.

No. 14. Supposed name Farber; age 35 years; 5 feet 6 inches high; had on person 2 pair dark pants; 1 checked and 2 wool shirts; 1 cassinet coat; 1 letter; cash $13.18; deceased had sandy whiskers.

No. 15. Richard Marshall (colored) 2d steward on America; age 25 years; 5 feet 8 inches in height.

No. 16. Burt Taylor (colored) age 46 years; 6 feet high.

No. 17. Unknown man (colored) age 25 years; 5 feet in height; had on person black pants, blue coat, calf boots, 1 lancet, 1 knife and comb.

No. 18. Miles Loffrom (colored); age 25 years; 5 feet 8 inches high.

No. 19. Thomas Cromer; age 23 years; 5 feet high.

No. 20. David Colliertes (colored); age 35 years; 5 feet high.

No. 21. ___ Elijah (colored), porter on steamer U. S.; age 35 years.

No. 22. Luke Burns (colored); age 47 years; 5 feet 6 inches high.

No. 23. John H. King (colored); age 20 years; 5 feet 10 inches high.

No. 24. Unknown woman (colored); age 18 years; 5 feet high with calico dress, black waist; 1 pair gloves; cash 3 cents.

No. 25. Unknown man (colored); age 25 years; 5 feet 6 inches high.

No. 26. Unknown man (colored); age 50 years; 5 feet 9 inches high; found on person 1 silver heart marked "J. I. H."

No. 27. Charly ___ (colored); age 40 years; 5 feet 10 inches high.

No. 28. Unknown man (colored); age 25 years; 5 feet 10 inches high with brown pants and red shirt.

No. 29. Charles W. Smith (colored); age 25 years; 5 feet 6 inches high.

No. 30. Edward Linder (colored); age 50 years; 5 feet 6 inches high.

No. 31. Unknown man; 5 feet 6 inches high, of about 180 pounds weight badly burned.

No. 32. Mrs. Griffin.

No. 33. Unknown lady with only part of a hoop skirt on person.

No. 34. Unknown man so badly burned as to be beyond description.

No. 35. Dowinie Zust, Italian, age 30 years; 5 feet 6 inches high.

No. 36. George W. Fannestock, age 50 years; 5 feet 8 inches high.

No. 37. ____ Zodine, had on is person note on Bank of Tennessee $10, Confederate script $20, National Bank $100, C. S. bills and currency $37.00; 1 gold ring.

No. 38. James Fields (colored); age 25 years; 5 feet 8 inches high.

No. 39. Unknown man (colored); age 18 years; 5 feet 4 inches high; Janes clothing.

No. 40. ___ Douglass (colored); age 13 years; 5 feet 4 inches high; Janes clothes.

No. 41. Unknown man; age 19 years; 4 feet 10 inches high; badly burned.

No. 42. Willis Floyd (colored); age 35 years; 6 feet high.

No. 43. Geo. Coble (colored); age 45 years; 5 feet 10 inches high.

No. 44. Unknown man, 5 feet 4 inches high; full set of teeth; badly burned.

No. 45. Unknown man, age 30 years; 5 feet 6 inches high; severely burned.

No. 46. H.H. Bunkhelder; age 40 years; 5 feet 4 inches high.

No. 47. Unknown man, Irish; age 30 years; 5 feet 8 inches high; Janes clothes.

No. 48. Hony Brenich; age 24 years; 5 feet 1 inch high; ring on left hand.

No. 49. Unknown female; age 15 or 20 years; 4 feet 10 inches high; badly charred.

No. 50. Unknown man (colored); age 30 years; 5 feet 8 inches high; with 2 pairs brown janes pants on; bed ticking blouse.

No. 51. Marlin McLermit age 19 years; 5 feet 8 inches high.

No. 52. Unknown man; 5 feet 10 inches high; weight 165 to 170 pounds.

No. 53. Unknown man; 5 feet 4 inches high; weight 150 pounds.

No. 54. Unknown man; age 70 years; 5 feet 8 inches high; weight 150 pounds.

AUTHOR'S NOTE

This book is primarily the compilation and summary of the previous work of two writers, Dr. Carl Bogardus (1977-80) of Warsaw, Kentucky, and Claude Brown (1956) of Switzerland County, Indiana, though their work was never published except in serial form in local newspapers. (See Selected Sources on page 91.)

Added information was found in newspaper reports of the events of that night at Rayl's Landing, from publications in the local Tri-State area, and as far-flung as Lawrence, Kansas; Concord, New Hampshire; New York; Philadelphia; and beyond. New facts were found in the memoir of Marcus Toney, the biography of Ole Bull and from Dan Back, steamboat historian.

Some of the material derived from these sources was found to be contradictory. For example, most sources agreed that these two steamboats made two stops on their nightly runs from Cincinnati to Louisville, and vice versa. One stop was at Madison, Indiana, but some of the references indicated the second stop was at Aurora, Indiana, while others stated it was Lawrenceburg, Indiana. Because whiskey was loaded onto the United States at this stop on this night, and Lawrenceburg was well known for its spirit distillation industry, beginning in 1847, this town was chosen as the correct location.

Also, Mary Johnson was listed by some references as being from Madison, Indiana, and others stated she was a Louisville, Kentucky girl. Eva Jones was variously reported as being from Tallahassee and Pensacola, and her mother's name in some references was Hattie, and in others Nellie.

Some survivors found to their consternation that newspaper articles had reported their deaths in the tragedy. Ole Bull's biographers, Haugen and Cai, claimed he and his troupe were going *downriver* that night, which would have been impossible if they were traveling from Louisville to their next engagement at Cincinnati.

Perhaps most unusual is the statement in *Way's Packet Directory*, 1848-1994, which one reader called "the Sine Qua Non for anyone studying the steamboats of the western waters," that the night of the disaster was "clear," which contradicts all the other sources concerning the weather on that night. Also, the same source differs from others as to the movements of the *United States* immediately following the collision.

These problems should not be surprising considering the emotional state of witnesses involved in those desperate moments of the disaster, the difficulty encountered by reporters trying to get to the scene and the frailties of human memory as time passes following a tragic incident.

The author wishes to thank Linda Weaver of Alcoa, Tennessee, retired writer and editor from the University of Tennessee, Knoxville, who formatted the manuscript for printing, designed both covers and gave valuable advice along the way.

Don Morrison
Maryville, Tennessee
April 2017

SELECTED SOURCES

1. Back, Dan, steamboat historian, West Chester, Ohio.

2. Bladen, Martha, Executive Director of the Switzerland County Historical Society and Museums, Vevay, Indiana.

3. Bogardus, Dr. Carl, *Rendezvous with Destiny*, serialized in *Gallatin County News*, 1977-1980. Full article available at the Warsaw, Kentucky, Public Library.

4. Brown, Barry, Reference Librarian and Historian at the Switzerland County Public Library, Vevay, Indiana.

5. Brown, Claude, *The Collision of the Steamers United States and America,* 1956, one chapter serialized in the Vevay newspaper. Full article available at the Switzerland County Public Library, Vevay, Indiana.

6. Burnham, Philip, *So Far From Dixie: Confederates in Yankee Prisons*, 2003. Includes Marcus Toney's

story of Civil War combat, incarceration in the Elmira Prison, and his experience as a passenger on the ill-fated *United States* on her last voyage.

7. Grayson, Frank, Jr., *Thrills of the Historic Ohio River*, 1924.

8. Harley, Timothy, *Moon Lore*, 2015.

9. Haugen, Einar & Cai, Camilla, *Ole Bull: Norway's Romantic Musician and Cosmopolitan Patriot,* 1993.

10. Indiana Postal History Society, *Switzerland County Postal History*, 2015.

11. Kern, Ellyn, editor, *1868 River Boat Collision Near County Shores*, *The Grapevine*, Switzerland County Historical Society Newsletter, Vol. 1 No. 2, November, 1989. Summary of the tragic accident.

12. Way, Frederick Jr., *Way's Packet Directory, 1848-1994.*

13. https://en.wikipedia.org/w/index.php?title=Guards (steamboat)&oldid=741558061

www.ingramcontent.com/pod-product-compliance
Lightning Source LLC
Chambersburg PA
CBHW020955030426
42339CB00005B/110